KIDS ASK ABOUT
SNAKES

 **HOW** do snakes move?

WHAT do snakes eat?

 **DO** snakes make good pets?

Written by Christopher Nicholas
Illustrated by Mike Maydak

An imprint of PHOENIX International Publications, Inc.
Chicago • London • Hamburg • Mexico City • Sydney

Visit us at SequoiaKidsBooks.com for bonus downloadable content

Photo credits © 2025 Shutterstock.com: Natalliya85; Vera Larina; Alan Tunnicliffe; Alex Stemmers; islandboy_stocker; Javi Aran

Published by Sequoia Children's Publishing,
an imprint of Sequoia Publishing & Media, LLC

Sequoia Publishing & Media, LLC,
a division of Phoenix International Publications, Inc.

8501 West Higgins Road, Chicago, Illinois 60631
34 Seymour Street, London W1H 7JE
Heimhuder Straße 81, 20148 Hamburg

© 2026 Sequoia Publishing & Media, LLC
First Published © 2023 Twin Sisters IP, LLC. All rights reserved.

CustomerService@PhoenixInternational.com

Sequoia Children's Publishing and associated logo are registered trademarks of Sequoia Publishing & Media, LLC.

Active Minds is a registered trademark of Phoenix International Publications, Inc.

All rights reserved. This publication may not be reproduced in whole or in part by any means without permission from the copyright owners. Permission is never granted for commercial purposes.

This book is sold subject to the condition that it shall not, by way of trade or otherwise, be lent, resold, hired out, or otherwise circulated without the publisher's prior consent in any form or binding or cover other than that in which it is published and without similar condition being imposed on the subsequent purchaser.

www.PhoenixInternational.com

Library of Congress Control Number: 2022906778

ISBN: 978-1-64269-461-1

KIDS ASK ABOUT SNAKES

TABLE OF CONTENTS

What is a snake?	4
How do snakes move?	5
How do snakes see?	6
How do snakes hear and smell?	7
Where do snakes live?	8
What types of environments do snakes live in?	9
What do snakes eat?	10
Which animals do snakes eat?	11
How do snakes catch and kill their food?	12
How do snakes poison their prey?	13
Why do snakes squeeze their prey?	14
How do snakes eat and digest their food?	16
How do snakes protect themselves?	18
What do different snakes do to protect themselves?	19
How are snakes born?	20
What happens when snakes grow up?	21
Did you know?	22
Do snakes make good pets?	24

WHAT is a snake?

Snakes are reptiles! So are lizards, turtles, alligators, and crocodiles. Snakes are cold-blooded. Their body temperature depends on the temperature of the environment around them. People are warm-blooded. Our body temperature stays at about 98.6°F (37°C) no matter where we are.

Scarlet kingsnake

HOW do snakes move?

Snakes don't have legs—so they can't walk! They have to glide on their bellies or move their bodies side to side to get where they want to go. A snake's body is covered with hard little plates called scales. A snake may look wet and slimy, but it is actually dry.

DID YOU KNOW?

Snakes often bask in the sun to warm themselves up, then hide in the shade to cool off.

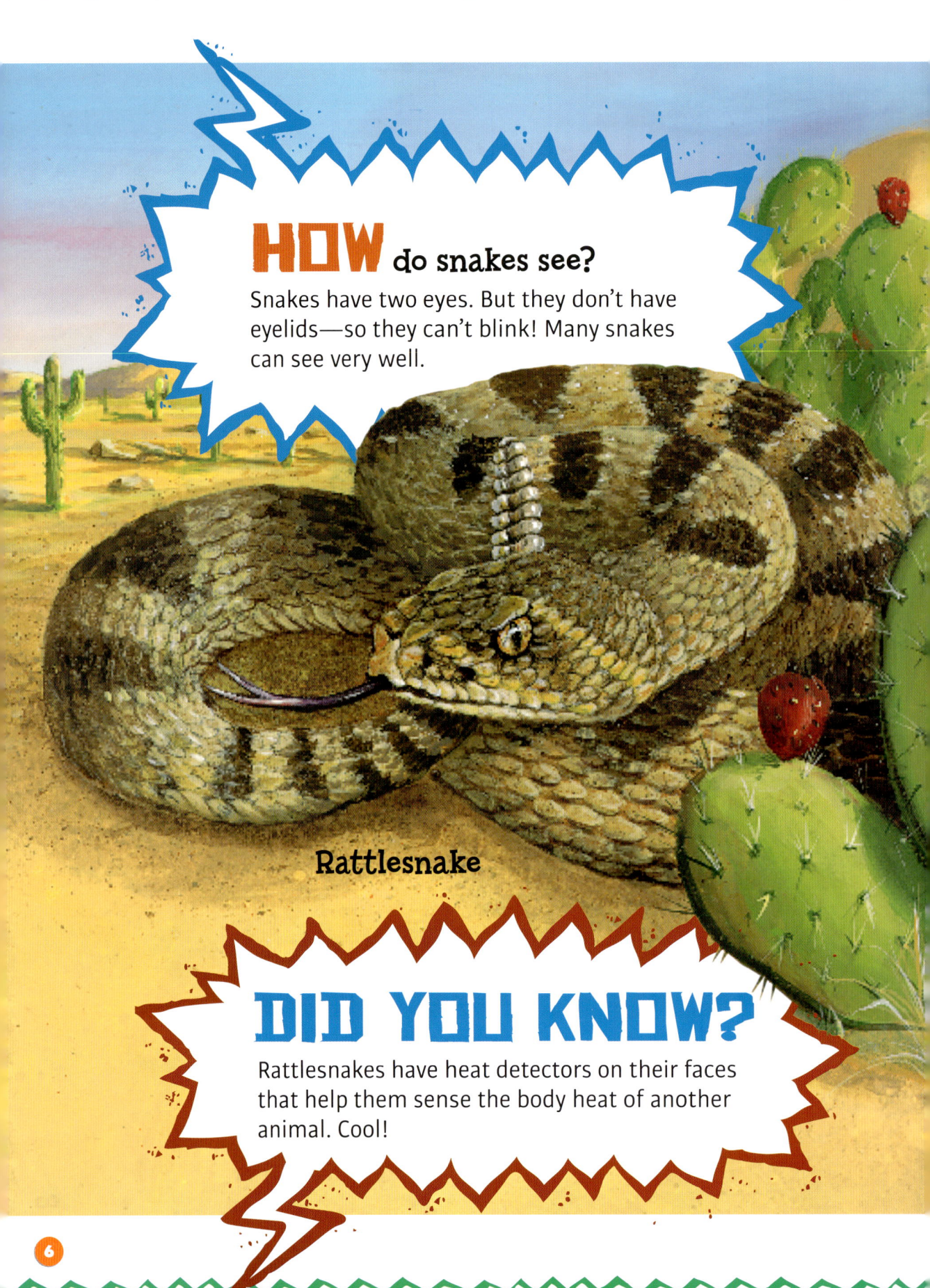

HOW do snakes see?

Snakes have two eyes. But they don't have eyelids—so they can't blink! Many snakes can see very well.

Rattlesnake

DID YOU KNOW?

Rattlesnakes have heat detectors on their faces that help them sense the body heat of another animal. Cool!

HOW do snakes hear and smell?

They don't have ears, but snakes can "hear" by feeling vibrations as they slither across the ground. And they can smell with the help of their forked tongue. One thing a snake does have is sharp teeth!

Sidewinder

SNAKES BODIES
- Scaly skin
- No legs
- No eyelids
- No ears
- Forked tongue
- Sharp teeth

WHERE do snakes live?

All over the world! But they especially like to be where it is warm. Sometimes they might even be in your own backyard!

Eastern ribbon snake

Green mamba

Sidewinder

DID YOU KNOW?

At the approach of the cold season, some snakes find a hole or den to sleep in until it becomes warm again.

WHAT types of environments do snakes live in?

Snakes can be found in jungles, deserts, swamps, and forests. They climb through the trees, hide in grass and among rocks, and glide across the sand. Some even swim in oceans, lakes, and rivers!

Banded sea snake

SNAKES LIVE IN...

- Jungles
- Deserts
- Swamps
- Forests
- Grass, rocks, trees, sand
- Oceans, lakes, rivers
- Underground

WHAT do snakes eat?

They eat meat! That's why they are called carnivores—a word that means meat-eaters. Most snakes feed on small animals. But larger snakes can eat big animals!

Copperhead

DID YOU KNOW?

Some snakes even eat other snakes!

WHICH animals do snakes eat?

Different types of snakes eat different animals, including insects, worms, frogs, lizards, mice, rats, and rabbits. Some snakes eat birds and larger animals.

Mexican milk snake

Asp viper

HOW do snakes catch and kill their food?

Snakes are sneaky! Sometimes they hide and wait for a meal to pass by. Other times they creep up on an animal—and attack with their sharp teeth!

HOW do snakes poison their prey?

Some snakes are poisonous. They use their big, hollow fangs to give victims a shot of deadly venom. One kind of cobra can blind animals by spitting venom into their eyes.

Cobra

WHY do snakes squeeze their prey?

Some snakes use their big, strong bodies to squeeze the life out of an animal. This is called constriction. That's where the boa constrictor got its name!

Emerald tree boa

HOW SNAKES GET FOOD
- Sharp teeth
- Poison
- Constriction

HOW do snakes eat and digest their food?

Snakes always swallow a meal whole—sometimes while it is still alive! It can take an hour to get a big animal into a snake's belly, and weeks to digest it. Snakes have very strong stomach juices that can even dissolve bones and teeth.

Ball python

SNAKES EATING AND DIGESTION

- Swallow meals whole
- Use specially hinged, wide-opening jaws
- Have strong stomach juices

DID YOU KNOW?

With its specially hinged jaws, a snake can swallow animals larger than its own head!

HOW do snakes protect themselves?

Any way they can! Snakes are great hunters, but sometimes they get hunted themselves. Large birds, crocodiles, and other animals love a tasty snake snack.

Sand viper

Coral snake

Rattlesnake

WHAT do different snakes do to protect themselves?

The rattlesnake will hiss loudly and rattle its tail to frighten enemies. The rubber boa curls into a ball and hides its head if attacked. The black mamba moves as fast as 7 miles (11 kilometers) per hour to escape predators. And the hognose snake rolls over and plays dead!

Rubber boa

Black mamba

HOW SNAKES PROTECT THEMSELVES

- Camouflage
- Bright warning colors
- Frightening sounds
- Curling up
- Playing dead
- Moving quickly

Hognose snake

HOW are snakes born?

Most snakes hatch from eggs. The eggs are tough and leathery, not brittle like bird eggs. Some snakes give birth to live babies! Newborn baby snakes can take care of themselves right away.

HOW SNAKES GROW UP

- May hatch from eggs or be born live
- Can care for themselves from birth
- Shed skin

WHAT happens when snakes grow up?

Just as you outgrow your clothes, snakes get too big for their scaly skins. Several times a year they have to shed, or peel, their skin off. It comes off all in one piece—just like a sock!

DID YOU KNOW?

Asian reticulated python
The Asian reticulated python is the longest snake—some reach lengths of 30 feet (9 m)!

Gaboon vipers have the largest fangs—up to 2 inches (5 cm) long!

Thread snake
The Barbados thread snake is the shortest snake. It is less than 5 inches (13 cm) long!

Green anaconda

Pound for pound, snakes have more muscle than any other animal.

The heaviest snake, the green anaconda, may weigh up to 500 pounds (227 kg)!

Indonesian flying snake

The Indonesian flying snake can glide through the air from tree to tree!

Sometimes snakes are born with two heads!

African rock python

The African rock python can live up to 2 years without eating.

We have 12 pairs of ribs; snakes have over 200 pairs!

Rough green snake

Snakes are long and skinny, so most, like this rough green snake, have only one working lung—they don't have room for two!

DO snakes make good pets?

It depends on you and your family. But a few types of snakes—like garter, king, and corn snakes—are easy to keep. And, if treated properly, snakes can be among the most interesting pets you'll ever have!